W9-CAW-604

DISCARD

McCordsville Elementary
Media Center

DISCARD

FORTVILLE - VERNON TWP.
PUBLIC LIBRARY
FORTVILLE, IN 46040

A New True Book

ALLIGATORS AND CROCODILES

By Lynn M. Stone

CHILDRENS PRESS®
CHICAGO

An American alligator enjoys the sun
with two turtle companions.

PHOTO CREDITS

American Museum of Natural History,
Department of Library Services—37
(trans. no. V/C 2583)

AP/Wide World Photos—43 (2 photos)

Cameramann International, Ltd.—29
(right), 33 (right), 35 (right), 39, 40 (2
photos)

© Barry Mansell—12 (left), 28

Root Resources—© Bill Glass; 7 (left);
© Stan Osolinski; 9, 35 (left); © Earl L.
Kubis; 13

© James P. Rowan—4, 20 (left), 33 (left),
45

Tom Stack & Associates—© Jeff Foott;
cover; © Rod Allin; 16 (top), 24 (right), 25,
26; © Bill Everitt; 18 (left); © John
Cancalosi; 8 (bottom left), 21, 32 (left);
© Cristopher Crowley; 16 (bottom);
© Kerry Givens; 24 (left); © Brian Parker;
31 (left), 32 (right); © Gary Milburn; 31
(right)

Lynn M. Stone—2, 6 (2 photos), 7 (right),
8 (top left, top & bottom right), 10, 12
(right), 15 (2 photos), 18 (right), 20
(right), 22, 29 (left), 42 (2 photos), 44 (2
photos)
Cover—American crocodile basking in
the sun, Jeff Foott

Library of Congress Cataloging-in-Publication Data

Stone, Lynn M.
  Alligators and crocodiles / by Lynn M. Stone
      p.   cm. — (A new true book)
  Includes index.
  Summary: Describes the physical characteristics,
behavior, habitats, and different species of alligators
and crocodiles.
    1. Alligators—Juvenile literature.
  2. Crocodiles—Juvenile literature.
  [1. Alligators. 2. Crocodiles.] I. Title.
QL666.C925S77   1989   89-9985
597.98—dc20   CIP
                                          AC

Copyright © 1989 by Childrens Press®, Inc.
All rights reserved. Published simultaneously in Canada.
Printed in the United States of America.
1 2 3 4 5 6 7 8 9 10 R 98 97 96 95 94 93 92 91 90 89

TABLE OF CONTENTS

Spanish explorers called the American alligator
el lagarto, which means "the lizard."

NOT QUITE A LIZARD

The first Spanish explorers to visit Florida found a strange, new animal. It was long and leathery. It had four short legs. It had long, flat jaws.

The Spaniards called the animal *el lagarto*, which means "the lizard." What the Spaniards had found was not quite a lizard, however. It was the American alligator.

Crocodile teeth (above) and
the "crooked, toothy smile"
of the alligator (right)

The alligator and its
cousin the crocodile are
related to lizards, but they
are smarter and bigger.
When their jaws are open,
alligators and crocodiles
show long rows of sharp
teeth.

Alligators and crocodiles have ridges and plates on their backs that look like metal armor. Their skin is used to make leather goods.

Alligators and crocodiles make up a group of water-loving animals called crocodilians. Crocodilians belong to a larger group of animals known as reptiles. The reptile family

Box turtle (above),
green snake (top right),
collared lizard (right), and
New Zealand tuatara (below)

includes turtles, snakes,
lizards, and the rare
tuatara of New Zealand.
Crocodilians are like
other reptiles. They have
scaly skin. They lay eggs

Alligators and crocodiles often rest with their huge jaws open. This helps the animals control their body temperature.

with shells, and they are cold-blooded.

The body temperature of a cold-blooded animal changes with its location. A reptile usually has to find sunshine to be warm. It must have shade to be cool.

Crocodiles are dangerous.

Crocodilians weigh from
just a few pounds to more
than 2,000 pounds. The
biggest of the crocodilians,
more than twenty feet in
length, are the giants of
the reptile world.

NATURE'S SUBMARINES

Alligators and crocodiles spend much of their lives in water. For swimming they have streamlined bodies and webbed feet, just as otters and ducks do. The tail is used like a paddle. It also steers the animal and gives it power in the water. A ten-foot crocodile has over five feet of tail!

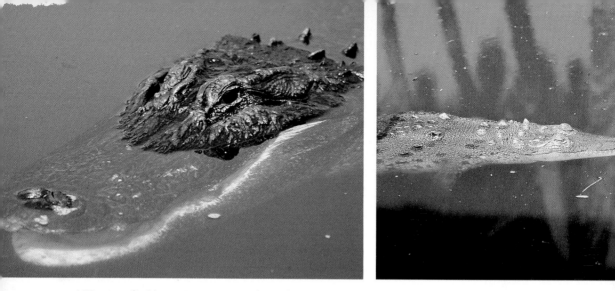

Alligator (left) and crocodile (right)

Crocodilians are nature's submarines. They can cruise on the surface of a lake or river or dive below.

When a crocodile or alligator dives, it is able to close its nose, throat, and ear openings. This keeps water from pouring into the animal.

On land crocodilians are awkward. Still, they have to come onto land to build nests, lay eggs, and rest. Often they crawl on their bellies. However, they can raise themselves on their feet and move quickly when they need to.

This alligator is fifteen feet long.

Crocodilians don't stray far from water. American alligators have been known to walk ten miles looking for water.

Most crocodiles and alligators live in very warm climates because cold weather slows them down. The animals that sometimes face cold weather burrow into mud for protection. Their body systems slow down, and they need no

Crocodilians stay near water.

food other than what is already in them. As soon as the air and the water temperatures warm, they become active again.

Active crocodiles and alligators are the noisiest of the reptiles. They grunt, hiss, growl, and roar.

15

With its mouth closed, the crocodile (above) shows many pairs of teeth. The alligator (below) does not show as many teeth.

CROCODILES AND ALLIGATORS

In many ways, alligators and crocodiles are alike. Still, there are differences. Scientists separate them according to differences in their skulls, scales, and teeth.

The crocodile's skull and jaws are narrower than the alligator's. When its jaws are shut, it has more teeth sticking out than an alligator does.

17

Crocodiles (left) like salt water.
Alligators (right) prefer fresh water.

Another difference
between crocodiles and
alligators is their choice of
homes. Many species of
crocodiles live in salt water.
On the other hand,
alligators are freshwater

reptiles. They rarely swim into salt water.

The only area in the United States where both alligators and crocodiles live is the southern tip of Florida. The American crocodile lives in the United States, Central America, and South America.

The American crocodile is large. It probably grows to twenty feet in length.

You will probably never see a wild crocodile. They are rare and shy.

The Nile crocodile (above) and
the mugger crocodile (right)
have been known to kill people.

Of the fifteen species of
crocodiles in the world
only three kinds have been
known to kill people. They
are the African Nile
crocodile, the saltwater
crocodile of Australia, and
the mugger crocodile of
Southeast Asia.

20

ALLIGATORS

FORTVILLE - VERNON TWP.
PUBLIC LIBRARY
FORTVILLE, IN 46040

Although American crocodiles are shy animals, alligators are not.

Alligators often have contact with people. When alligators become used to

Although it looks awkward, the alligator can attack suddenly.

people, they lose their fear of them. Fearless alligators can be very dangerous to people.

Alligators are not as active as crocodiles. In fact, they appear to be slow, sleepy animals. They

A young alligator takes a nap in the sun.

are usually seen floating quietly in the water or resting on a muddy shore.

Nevertheless, alligators can move surprisingly fast, and they can be very dangerous.

Alligators can grow to be twelve or fourteen feet long and weigh several hundred pounds. Most alligators are much smaller than that. An eight-foot alligator is unusual in the wild.

The alligator's webbed feet are used for swimming. Its claws (above) are used for digging.

Alligators sometimes dig water holes in the mud of swamps and marshes. When the dry season begins, these water holes may hold the only deep fresh water around.

CROCODILIAN NESTS

When crocodilians are seven or more years old, they mate. The female lays eggs.

Some crocodiles dig a hole in loose soil, lay their eggs, and bury them. Others lay eggs in nest mounds of sticks, dirt, and leaves.

Crocodiles and alligators lay eggs.

rdsville Elementary
Media Center

Crocodiles usually lay between thirty and fifty eggs.

American alligators build mounded nests on shores or in swamps. They lay from twenty-five to seventy eggs.

A female alligator guards its nest.

Mother crocodiles remain
near their nest. The eggs
stay warm in the soil where
they are buried. They take
from nine to ten weeks
to hatch.

Some mothers guard their
nests much more closely
than others. Females at
their nests can be very
fierce. It is never wise
for anyone to come too
close to a nest.

Baby alligator hatching

The babies make sounds
as they hatch. The mothers
may help their young to
dig out of the nest.

Many eggs never have a
chance to hatch. Several
different animals dig into
the nests and steal eggs.

Great blue heron (left) and a
flock of white herons (right)

The adult animals have
no natural enemies. Baby
crocodiles and alligators,
however, are eaten by
hunting animals such as
the heron. Strangely, adult
crocodilians sometimes
eat their young.

29

WHERE DO ALLIGATORS AND CROCODILES LIVE?

Crocodilians live in the warmer regions of southern North America, South America, Southeast Asia, Australia, and a tiny part of China. They are almost always in or near water. The gavial, a crocodilian that lives in India, has a long, narrow snout with 100 teeth.

Alligators have some very close relatives in

The gavial (left) lives in India and the caiman (above) lives in South America.

South America. They are called caimans.

Alligators and caimans are freshwater species. The American alligator lives in rivers, lakes, and swamps in nine of the southeastern United States. The Chinese alligator lives

Saltwater crocodile (above) and
the Cuban crocodile (right)

only in the Yangtze River
valley of central China.
Caimans live throughout
South America.

The smallest crocodile
species often live in fresh
water too. The small
Cuban crocodile lives only
in Cuba's Zapata Swamp.

In Florida, the Big Cypress Swamp (left) and the boardwalk in Everglades National Park (right) are good places to see alligators and crocodiles.

Most of the larger crocodiles live in salt water. The Nile, American, and saltwater crocodiles are at home in salty bays and in the mouths of rivers. Crocodiles don't like waves; they rarely travel in open ocean water.

CROCODILIAN HUNTERS

Crocodilians are hunters that eat other animals.

Crocodiles and alligators can kill almost any animal they find. But they usually eat smaller prey—birds, turtles, snakes, fish.

Crocodilians hunt in the water. Their hunting is helped by good eyes and ears. Sometimes they lunge from the water to

Only the eyes and nostrils of the alligator (left) appear above the water.
The New Guinea crocodile (right) eats a fish dinner on land.

grab an animal, such as a
deer, that steps in shallow
water to drink. More often,
they drift like floating
logs toward their prey.
Both alligators and
crocodiles can float so
that only their eyes and

nostrils rise above the water. It is hard for the prey animal to see these hunters—until it is too late. Crocodilians also attack by swimming up from beneath the surface.

Crocodilians do not have to hunt every day. A big meal can last them for several days.

Alligators and crocodiles cannot chew their food. They have to tear their prey into bite-size gulps.

ENDANGERED CROCODILIANS

Almost all of the world's twenty-five species of crocodilians are endangered.

The crocodilians had ancestors that lived at the time of the dinosaurs. Crocodilians, then, have survived for millions of years. But they are in

Skeleton of the first known ancestor of the crocodile is on display at the American Museum of Natural History in New York City.

serious trouble now. The Siamese crocodile, the Chinese alligator, and the Cuban crocodile are some of the world's rarest animals. Only Johnston's crocodile of Australia and the American alligator seem to be safe from extinction.

Crocodilians have disappeared for many reasons. Thousands have been killed because people are afraid of them. Most of the horror stories

about them aren't true.
Still, many people believe
the worst about these
animals.

Many thousands of
alligators and crocodiles
have been killed for their
skins. Their skin is made
into fine leather.

A New Guinea
trader measures
a crocodile skin
for payment.

In New Guinea, artists carve the crocodile on statues and on the prows of their canoes.

Most of the world's endangered crocodilians live in poor countries. These countries are trying to make life better for their people. Actions that help people do not always help wild animals. If a nation needs more land for farming, it can drain a swamp. Many of the animals that lived in the swamp, such as the crocodilians, vanish. They cannot live without water.

Several nations have tried to protect these animals from being hunted.

The value of crocodilian skins has caused people to start alligator and crocodile farms. There the animals are raised for their skins.

Alligator farms (left) and restaurants
serving alligator meat attract tourists in Florida.

Until quite recently, the
American alligator was an
endangered animal in the
United States. Now the
number has grown so much
that Florida and Louisiana
have started alligator hunts.
Alligators have become

Due to overpopulation of alligators in Florida and Louisiana, people are allowed to hunt them (left). Searching for new bodies of water, alligators such as the 12-foot, 500-pound male shown above represent a danger to people.

a problem in some places. Stray alligators have been removed from lawns, garages, golf courses, and swimming pools.

The American crocodiles have probably never been common in the United States. But the United

Researchers study crocodiles in
this refuge at Key Largo, Florida.

States is working hard to
protect them. The U.S. Fish
and Wildlife Service has
a 7,000-acre refuge for
crocodiles in Key Largo.

The people at the refuge
treat the crocodiles with
caution. All crocodiles
should be treated

Siamese
crocodile

carefully. Very few are man-eaters, but all of them can bite.

Alligators and crocodiles should be treated with respect. They are a living bridge to the Age of Dinosaurs.

WORDS YOU SHOULD KNOW

alligator(AL • ih • gay • ter) — a large reptile that has a long tail, short legs, and a short, flat head

awkward(AWK • werd) — moving without ease or smoothness; clumsy

burrow(BER • roh) — to dig out a hole in the ground

caiman(KAY • min) — a reptile that looks much like an alligator

crocodile(KRAH • kuh • dyle) — a large reptile that has short legs, a long tail, and a long, narrow head

crocodilian(krah • kuh • DIL • ee • yan) — one of a group of reptiles like the alligator and crocodile, having long jaws, a long tail, and short legs

dinosaur(DYE • nuh • sore) — any of a group of extinct animals that dominated the earth many millions of years ago; some grew to enormous size

endangered(en • DAIN • jird) — in danger of dying out

extinct(ex • TINKT) — no longer living

gavial(GAV • ee • yal) — a crocodilian that is found in India

leathery(LEH • ther • ee) — like leather; smooth, tough, and flexible

lizard(LIHZ • erd) — an air-breathing, cold-blooded animal (such as a snake) that is covered with scales or bony plates and that has very short legs or no legs at all

predator(PREHD • ah • ter) — an animal that kills and eats other animals

prey(PRAY) — an animal that is hunted and eaten by another animal

range(RAYNGE) — the region in which a plant or animal can be found in the wild

refuge(REH • fyooj) — a safe place where animals can live without being harmed by people

reptile(REHP • tyle) — a cold-blooded animal that has a backbone and that has very short legs or no legs at all

streamlined(STREEM • lyned) — having a shape that allows easy movement through air or water

submarine(SUHB • muh • reen) — a boat that can travel underwater

tuatara(too • ah • TAHR • rah) — a very ancient, slow-moving, medium-sized reptile of New Zealand that looks like a lizard

INDEX

About the Author

Lynn M. Stone was born and raised in Meriden, Connecticut. He received his undergraduate degree from Aurora College in Illinois and his master's degree from Northern Illinois University. Once a teacher in Sarasota, Florida, Mr. Stone currently teaches English to junior high school students in the West Aurora Public School system.

A free-lance wildlife photographer and journalist, Lynn has had his work appear in many publications including National Wildlife, Ranger Rick, Oceans, Country Gentleman, Animal Kingdom, and International Wildlife. He has also contributed to Time-Life, National Geographic, Audubon Field Guide, and Hallmark Cards publications.

Many of Lynn Stone's photographs have been used in the New True Books published by Childrens Press.